MCDOUGLE ELEMENTARY
10410 Kansack Lane
Houston, Texas 77086

A Kid's Guide to Drawing the Presidents of the United States of America™

How to Draw the Life and Times of
Woodrow Wilson

Melody S. Mis

The Rosen Publishing Group's
PowerKids Press™
New York

To Bruce, wherever you are

Published in 2006 by The Rosen Publishing Group, Inc.
29 East 21st Street, New York, NY 10010

Copyright © 2006 by The Rosen Publishing Group, Inc.

All rights reserved. No part of this book may be reproduced in any form without permission in writing from the publisher, except by a reviewer.

First Edition

Editor: Jennifer Way
Layout Design: Ginny Chu
Photo Researcher: Jeffrey Wendt

Illustration Credits: All illustrations by Elana Davidian.

Photo Credits: Cover, p. 28 © Getty Images; pp. 4, 20 Library of Congress Prints and Photograph Division; p. 7 © Corbis; p. 8 Courtesy of The Library of Virginia; p. 9 Benton Nelson; p. 10 © Lake County Museum/Corbis; p. 14 © Alan Goldsmith/Corbis; p. 16 www.ronwadebuttons.com; p.18 Photographs and Prints Division, Schomburg Center for Research in Black Culture, The New York Public Library, Astor, Lenox and Tilden Foundations; p. 22 © Hulton-Deutsch Collection/Corbis; p. 24 © Ted Spiegel/Corbis; p. 26 (top) the Ohio Historical Society; p. 26 (bottom) Library of Congress Manuscripts Division.

Library of Congress Cataloging-in-Publication Data

Mis, Melody S.
  How to draw the life and times of Woodrow Wilson / Melody S. Mis.— 1st ed.
      p. cm. — (A kid's guide to drawing the presidents of the United States of America)
  Includes index.
  ISBN 1-4042-3004-1 (library binding)
  1. Wilson, Woodrow, 1856–1924—Juvenile literature. 2. Presidents—United States—Biography—Juvenile literature. 3. Drawing—Technique—Juvenile literature. I. Title. II. Series.
  E767.M47 2006
  973.91'3'092—dc22

2005002788

Printed in China

Contents

1	Thomas Woodrow Wilson	4
2	The Twenty-eighth President	6
3	Wilson's Virginia	8
4	Wilson's Birthplace	10
5	Princeton University	12
6	Governor of New Jersey	14
7	The 1912 Presidential Campaign	16
8	Wilson and Race Relations	18
9	The United States Enters World War I	20
10	The 1918 Flu Epidemic	22
11	The Nobel Peace Prize	24
12	Suffrage for Women	26
13	Wilson's Legacy	28
	Timeline	30
	Glossary	31
	Index	32
	Web Sites	32

Thomas Woodrow Wilson

Thomas Woodrow Wilson was a lawyer, a college president, a governor, and one of America's greatest presidents. He also helped create the League of Nations, an organization to support world peace.

Wilson was born on December 28, 1856, in Staunton, Virginia. He was the third of four children born to Reverend Joseph Wilson and Janet Woodrow Wilson. Reverend Wilson taught his son that it was important to think quickly, to speak clearly, and to use the correct words to express himself. These lessons would help Wilson when he entered politics.

At age 16, Wilson entered Davidson College in North Carolina, where he studied for one year. In 1875, he enrolled at Princeton University in Princeton, New Jersey. Wilson graduated near the top of his class in 1879. After graduation he studied law at the University of Virginia in Charlottesville, Virginia. In 1882, Wilson opened a law office in Atlanta,

Georgia. On a trip to Rome, Georgia, in 1883, he met Ellen Louise Axson, whom he married two years later.

In 1883, Wilson entered Johns Hopkins University in Baltimore, Maryland. Wilson taught history and government at two other colleges before he was hired to teach at Princeton University in 1890. In 1902, Wilson was elected president of Princeton University. He held that post until 1910, when he was elected governor of New Jersey. While he was governor, the Democratic Party chose Wilson to run for president. Wilson won the 1912 election to become the nation's twenty-eighth president.

You will need the following supplies to draw the life and times of Woodrow Wilson:

✓ A sketch pad   ✓ An eraser   ✓ A pencil   ✓ A ruler

These are some of the shapes and drawing terms you need to know:

Horizontal Line	——	Squiggly Line	〜〜
Oval	⬭	Trapezoid	⏢
Rectangle	▭	Triangle	△
Shading	▬	Vertical Line	│
Slanted Line	/	Wavy Line	〜

The Twenty-eighth President

On March 4, 1913, Woodrow Wilson began the first of his two presidential terms. A year into his first term, in August 1914, Wilson's wife, Ellen, died. A year and a half later, Wilson married Edith Galt.

In 1914, World War I began in Europe. The United States stayed neutral until March 1917, when German submarines attacked American ships. This caused Wilson to declare war against Germany. After Germany surrendered in 1918, Wilson made a speech in which he proposed an end to the war. This was his Fourteen Points speech. His most important point was the creation of the League of Nations.

During his presidency Wilson passed a law that led to the eight-hour workday that most Americans enjoy today. Wilson also passed three amendments to the U.S. Constitution. The Seventeenth Amendment stated that U.S. senators were to be elected by the people instead of by state legislatures. The Eighteenth Amendment banned alcohol, and the Nineteenth Amendment gave women the right to vote.

In this undated photograph, Woodrow Wilson is riding in a parade. The men walking near Wilson are Secret Service agents. Their job is to protect the president when he is in public. Wilson rode in many parades, such as when he was sworn into office.

GRAY. L.A.

⑦

Wilson's Virginia

A bust of Woodrow Wilson stands in the rotunda of Virginia's capitol building in Richmond.

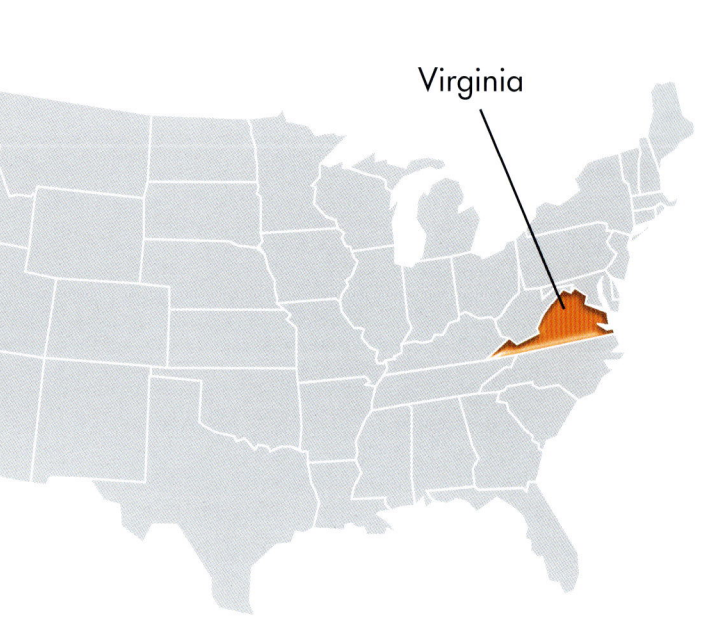

Map of the United States of America

Woodrow Wilson lived in Staunton, Virginia, for only two years, but he loved his hometown and visited it often. After Wilson died in 1924, Virginia honored him by naming a bridge after him. The bridge crosses the Potomac River from Maryland to Washington, D.C., and then to Virginia. The state also displays his bust in the rotunda of the capitol building in Richmond. A bust is a sculpture of a person's head and shoulders. The University of Virginia in Charlottesville honored Wilson by naming their Department of Politics after him. It has become one of the school's most popular departments.

Woodrow Wilson is one of three presidents who are buried inside a church. He is also the only president who is buried in Washington, D.C., which is just across the Potomac River from Virginia. He died on February 3, 1924, and is buried at the National Cathedral in Washington, D.C. A decorative glass and stone window in the cathedral, or church, memorializes Wilson by showing events from his life. It is open to the public.

This is Woodrow Wilson's tomb, or grave, in the National Cathedral in Washington, D.C. He is the only president who is buried at this location. The stained glass windows in the background illustrate events from Wilson's life.

Wilson's Birthplace

Woodrow Wilson was born on December 28, 1856, in Staunton, Virginia. The Wilsons lived in the home shown here. The First Presbyterian Church had provided the home because Wilson's father was the church's pastor.

In 1858, the Wilsons moved to Georgia, but Wilson visited his family in Staunton during his childhood. After Wilson's death in 1924, his birthplace home was sold to the Woodrow Wilson Birthplace Foundation. The group turned it into a memorial. In 1941, President Franklin D. Roosevelt named Wilson's birthplace as a "shrine to freedom." The home was listed as a national historic landmark in 1965. Today Wilson's birthplace is a museum and open to the public. The museum houses items from Wilson's family and his presidency. The Woodrow Wilson Library is also located on the grounds. There people can find out more about Wilson.

1

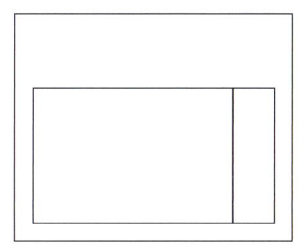

You will be drawing Wilson's birthplace. Draw a large rectangle. Make two smaller rectangles inside the first one. These will be your guides.

2

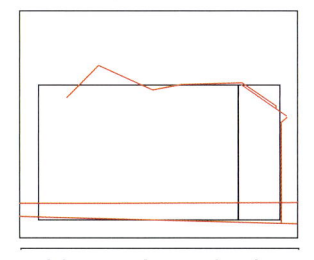

Add two slanted lines along the bottom. These will be your guides for drawing the fence. Then use slanted lines to make the side and start the roof of the house.

3

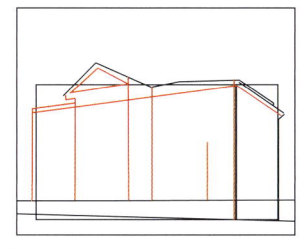

Using slanted horizontal lines and vertical lines, draw the front of the house. Add a triangle to the roof.

4

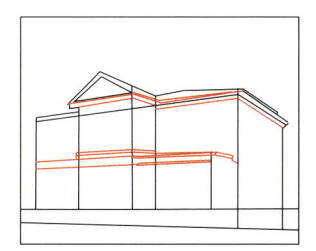

Erase the rectangular guides you made in step 1. Add horizontal, vertical, and slanted lines to the house as shown. These will be the edges of the roof and the porch.

5

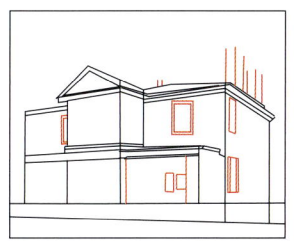

Using rectangular shapes and straight lines, add six windows. Notice that the windows on the left are partly hidden. Add eight vertical lines to the roof. These will be the chimneys.

6

Draw the tops of the chimneys. Draw vertical lines for the columns on the front of the house. Add the details for the porch and the side of the house as shown.

7

Draw a tree in the yard using crooked lines. Using vertical and slanted lines, draw the fence and the posts around the tree. Add details to the windows and chimneys. Add a window.

8

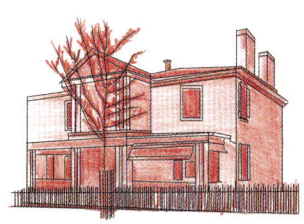

Erase the rectangular guide you made in step 1. Finish by adding detail and shading. Notice where the shading is the darkest, such as the inside of the windows. Nice work!

Princeton University

In 1875, Woodrow Wilson entered Princeton University in Princeton, New Jersey. The university's seal is shown here. Wilson studied political science and graduated in 1879.

After Princeton, Wilson went to law school. In 1882, he opened up a law practice. The next year he decided to go back to school to become a law professor. In 1885, Wilson graduated from Johns Hopkins University. He taught at two different colleges before Princeton hired him to teach law and politics in 1890. Wilson was a popular professor. He was chosen to be the university's president in 1902.

As Princeton's president Wilson put into place a new system of undergraduate studies that is used today at most colleges. His system ensured that students would have a well-rounded education. Wilson's success as Princeton's president got the attention of the Democratic Party of New Jersey, which nominated him for governor of New Jersey in the 1910 election.

1. Begin your drawing of Princeton's shield by making a rectangular guide. Draw a vertical line down the center with two horizontal lines crossing it. These lines will be your guides.

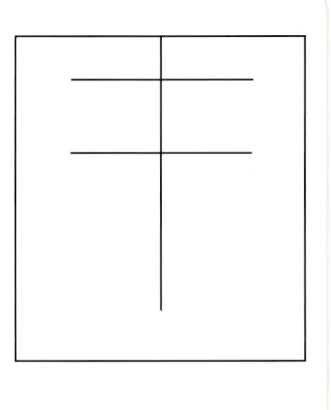

2. Add a curved line on each side of the shield. These lines meet at the bottom of the vertical guide as shown. Draw four slanted lines. They form upside-down V's.

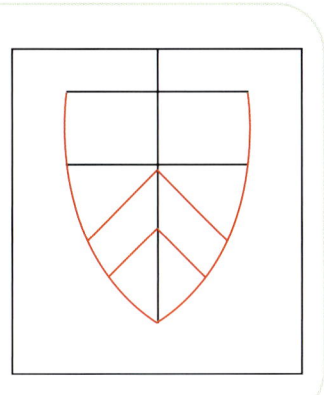

3. Add two curved lines along the top of the shield. Draw a rectangular guide for the book. Add four small rectangles next to the book guide. These four rectangles should all be the same size.

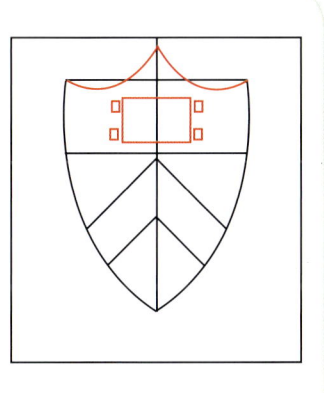

4. Erase the vertical guide you made in step 1. Draw three horizontal lines across the bottom of the rectangle. Add lines to the small rectangles and to the bottom of the book.

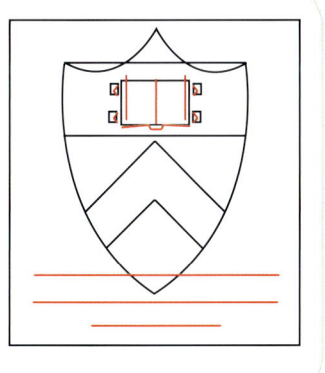

5. Erase extra lines. Add small lines along the horizontal lines you drew in step 4. Add lines to the book. In the book write the words "VET TES EN" on the left side and "NOV TAM TVM" on the right side. The V's are U's in Latin.

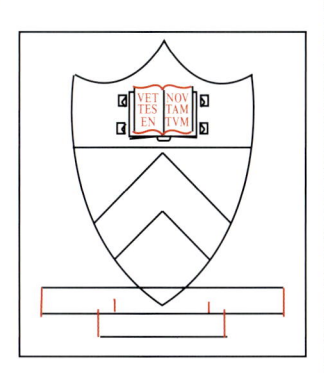

6. Add the curved lines along the bottom to make the curled ribbon beneath the shield. Use the horizontal and vertical lines as guides for this shape.

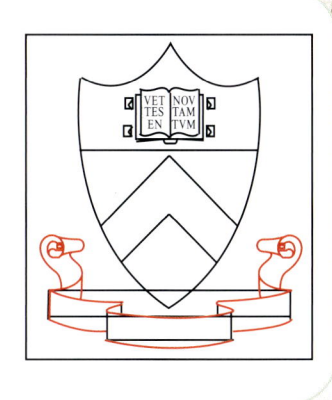

7. Erase the ribbon guides and the rectangular guide. Erase extra lines in the book and the four small shapes around the book. Write the words "DEI SVB NVMINE VIGET" on the ribbon.

8. Finish your drawing with shading and detail. Shade the top section and the slanted lines dark. Great job!

Governor of New Jersey

During his campaign for governor in 1910, Woodrow Wilson promised to change New Jersey's government. He wanted the state to be run more honestly. He won the election and became governor.

Wilson served as governor in the New Jersey capitol in Trenton. The capitol's famous dome is shown here. Because he was not an experienced politician, the Democratic Party leaders thought that they would be able to control Wilson. Wilson surprised them by being an effective governor who would not be controlled by his party. As governor, Wilson passed several laws that he hoped would make the state government work better for the people of New Jersey.

Wilson's progressive ideas made him popular in New Jersey and soon gained him national attention. The national Democratic Party noticed Wilson's growing popularity and nominated him to be the party's candidate in the 1912 presidential race.

1

You will be drawing the dome of the New Jersey capitol. Begin by drawing a large rectangle. Inside that rectangle draw two ovals and two rectangles as shown. These will be your guide shapes for the drawing.

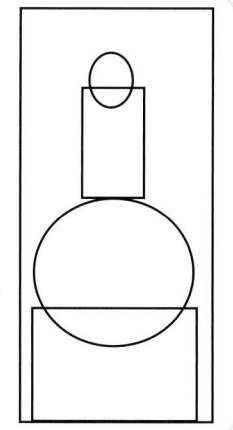

2

Draw curved lines on the bottom rectangular shape. In the smaller rectangle on top, add slanted lines, a square, and a small rectangle. These will be your guide shapes for the shape of the tower.

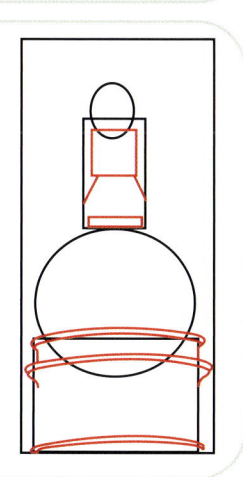

3

Add curved lines for the two domes using the oval guides you made in step 1. Then add more curved lines in the two rectangular sections.

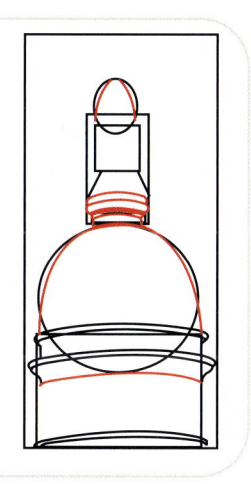

4

Draw a small oval on the top. This will be your guide for making the top shape on the dome. Add lines inside the guide shapes you made inside the rectangle in step 2. Draw curved lines on the larger dome.

5

Erase the guidelines from steps 1 and 2. Inside the small oval guide you made in step 4, add the shape shown. Add curved lines to the tower. Next use vertical and slanted lines for the columns on the dome.

6

Erase the oval guide you made in step 4. Add vertical lines to the tower. Draw small circles for windows. Add curved vertical lines to the lower part of the dome. Add a horizontal curved line to the part beneath the dome.

7

Erase the rectangular guides. Finish the drawing by adding shading. Shade the columns, the dome, and the inside of the windows dark. Great job!

The 1912 Presidential Campaign

Four candidates, representing four different political parties, ran in the 1912 presidential race. The Democrats' nominee was Woodrow Wilson. Conservative Republicans backed President William Taft, and progressive Republicans backed former president Theodore Roosevelt. Eugene Debs was the Socialist Party's candidate.

Wilson knew that the race would really be between him and Roosevelt, because they were the most popular candidates. Wilson traveled across the country to give speeches. There was neither television nor radio at this time, so Wilson handed out pins, like the one here, to advertise his candidacy.

Roosevelt had lost some of his popularity since his presidency. Some people thought he was too quick to use the military to solve problems. Wilson made people feel safer because he seemed to be a more careful leader. In November 1912, Wilson won the election to become the nation's twenty-eighth president.

1 You will be drawing a Wilson 1912 campaign pin. Begin by drawing a rectangular guide. Inside the rectangle draw a circle and two smaller ovals.

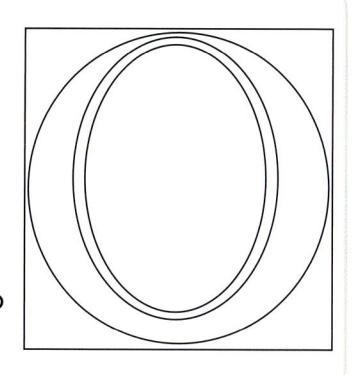

2 Next draw a smaller oval shape inside the ovals you drew in step 1. This oval will be your guide for drawing Wilson's face. Add curved lines for the details between the circle and the oval.

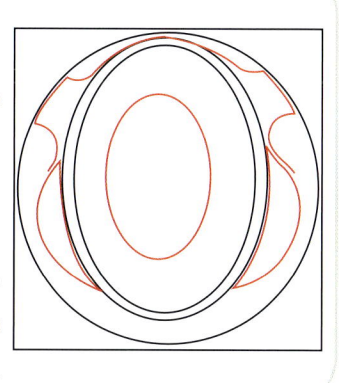

3 Draw the shapes of Wilson's hair, ear, and shoulders, using the guide shape you made in step 2. Add straight lines that will be your guides for drawing the eyes, nose, and mouth.

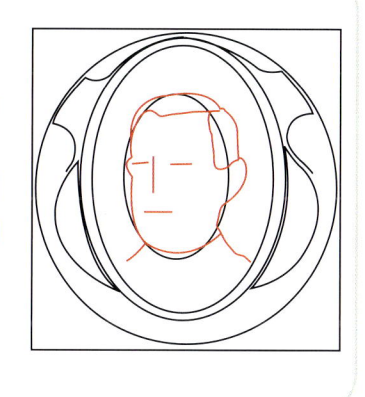

4 Draw the eyes using almond shapes. Add the nose using the guides you made in step 3. Add details to the chin and curved lines for the eyebrows. Erase the oval guide you made for the head.

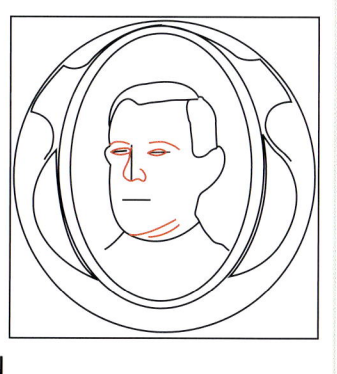

5 Using curved and wavy lines, add the details to the ear and the hair. Draw small circles for the eye's pupils. Draw the mouth using the guide from step 3. Add the outline of the clothes.

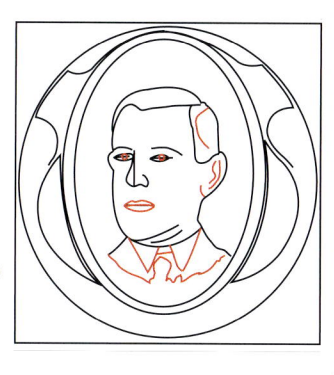

6 Erase the face guides. Add stars to the sides as shown. Draw vertical lines for the stripes. Using curved lines draw the leaf shapes along the side of the pin.

7 Add lines to the leaf shapes you drew in step 6. Erase the large rectangular guide you made in step 1.

8 Finish the drawing of the button by adding shading. Nice job!

Wilson and Race Relations

Many African Americans had supported Woodrow Wilson during the 1912 election, because they had hoped he would make reforms that would make their lives better. When Wilson allowed for the segregation of government workers, African Americans became angry. Segregation is the act of keeping certain people apart from others.

An African American leader named William Trotter, shown here, met with Wilson in November 1914, to protest this segregation. Wilson said he believed that segregation was needed to stop the problems that occurred between white and African American government workers. Trotter was angry that Wilson believed segregation was the only solution. When he left his meeting with Wilson, he spoke to newspaper reporters on the steps of the White House. Trotter's speech made Wilson angry, but he did not change his policy. Wilson's inability to improve race relations is one major area in which he failed as a president.

1

You will be drawing William Trotter. Begin by drawing a large rectangle. Add an oval and two slanted lines. These will be guides for the head and shoulders.

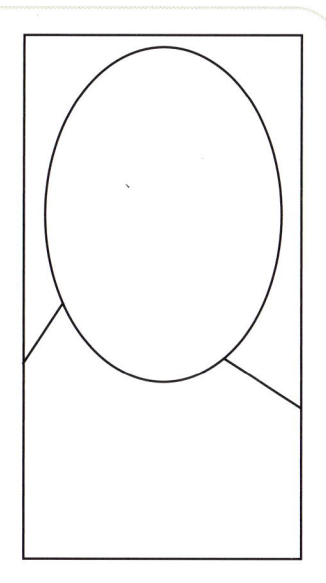

2

Draw an oval guide for the ear. Using straight lines add the guides for the eyes, nose, and mouth. Draw two slanted lines for guides for the jacket.

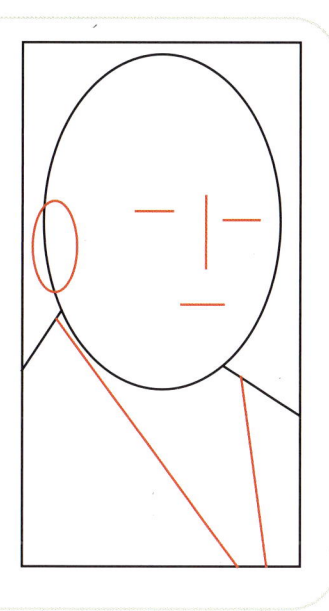

3

Using squiggly lines draw the outline of the hair. Using curved lines draw the outline of the face and ear. Draw the outline of the jacket using the guidelines you made in steps 1 and 2.

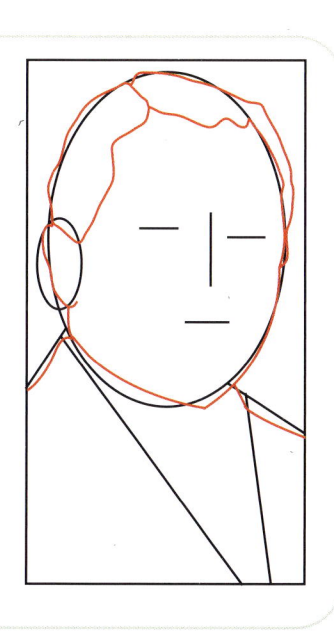

4

Erase the head and ear guidelines. Use curved lines to draw the eyes and the nose. Using straight lines and curved lines, draw the jacket, vest, and shirt. Add two curved lines for the eyebrows.

5

Erase extra lines. Add detail to the ear. Draw two small circles inside the eyes for the irises. Using curved lines add the mustache, the mouth, and the chin. Draw the tie and the buttonhole on the jacket using curved lines.

6

Erase the mouth guidelines and the rectangle you drew in step 1. Finish with shading. Great work!

The United States Enters World War I

On April 2, 1917, Woodrow Wilson asked Congress for a declaration of war against Germany. This meant the United States would enter World War I.

The war had begun in Europe in 1914. The fighting was between the Central Powers and the Allied Powers. The Central Powers included Germany and Austria-Hungary. The Allied Powers included Great Britain, France, and Russia. For nearly three years the United States was neutral. The promise to stay neutral was one of the reasons Wilson was reelected in 1916. The next year, however, he declared war because German submarines were sinking American ships.

Posters, like the one above, were used to encourage men to join the armed forces. American soldiers were sent to Europe, where they fought alongside the Allied armies to win the war. The war ended on November 11, 1918. In remembrance of this event, Wilson proclaimed November 11 a national holiday, which we now call Veterans Day.

1 You will be drawing James Montgomery Flagg's famous army poster. Begin by drawing a large rectangle. Add a small circle for the head guide. Make two straight lines for the body guidelines.

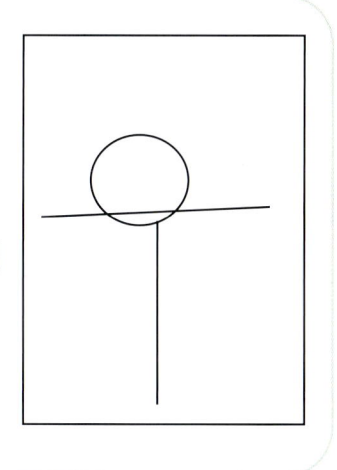

2 Draw slanted lines for the arm guidelines. Add ovals around these guides for the arms. Add a circular guide for the hand. Draw slanted lines to make guides for the hat.

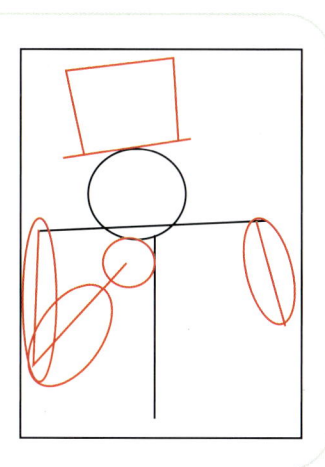

3 Using curved lines draw the hat inside the guide. Draw straight lines for guides for the eyes, nose, and mouth.

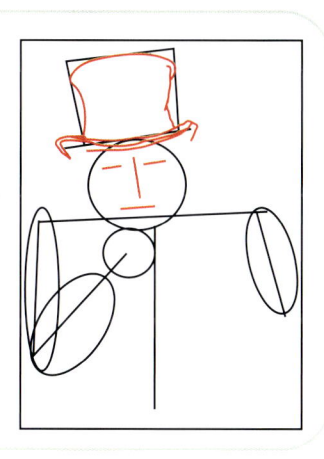

4 Add the band around the hat using a curved line. Draw stars on the band using straight lines. Add squiggly lines for the hair and the outline of the face.

5 Erase the circular guide and the hat guide. Using the face guides, draw the eyes, nose, and mouth. Draw the coat with squiggly lines. Add another squiggly line to start the beard. Outline the hand.

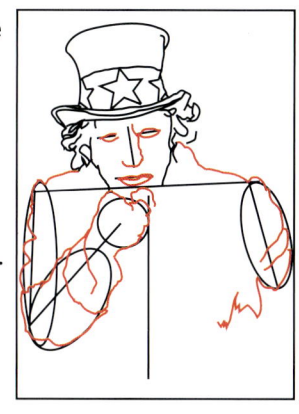

6 Erase extra lines. Using squiggly lines add the eyebrows. Add lines to the face. Draw small circles for the pupils in the eyes. Draw the hand inside the outline. Add the coat and tie.

7 Add the remaining lines to the clothes. Notice how the lines look like the folds in the clothes. Add lines to the hand. Draw the beard.

8 Erase the rectangular guide you made in step 1. Finish up the drawing by adding shading. Nice work!

The 1918 Flu Epidemic

While Woodrow Wilson was worried about the American lives that were being lost in the war, an epidemic spread quickly and began to claim the lives of Americans at home. An epidemic occurs when a serious illness spreads quickly to a large number of people. The flu epidemic began in March 1918, at an army camp in Kansas. More than 100 men became sick within a few hours.

The flu even spread to the battlefields of Europe. American soldiers had unknowingly brought the illness with them. By the end of 1918, the flu had spread from the United States to Europe and into Africa, India, and Asia, before it suddenly disappeared.

People were taken to hospitals in ambulances like the one here, but doctors did not have the medicine to cure the flu. Millions of people caught it. Even President Wilson got the flu, but he recovered from it. The flu killed more than 600,000 Americans, making it the worst epidemic in U.S. history.

1

You will be drawing an ambulance that was used during the flu epidemic. Begin by drawing a large rectangle. Inside draw two smaller rectangles. These will be your guides.

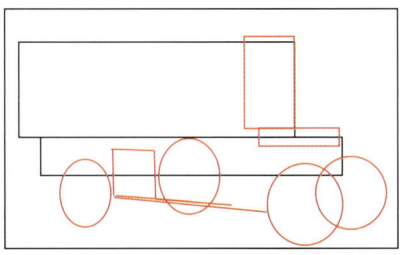

2

Draw two circles and two ovals for the wheels. Draw rectangles for guides for the window, side, and hood. Add slanted lines along the bottom. Add the shape between the back ovals.

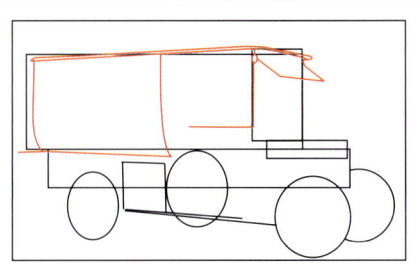

3

Using slanted lines draw the roof and the side of the car. Add more slanted lines for the window shade. Erase the lines that go through the front wheels.

4

Erase extra lines. Add the back tire. Add rectangle guides for the windows. Add curved lines to the wheels. Draw slanted lines on the roof of the car. Add the steering wheel.

5

Erase extra lines. Add circles and curved lines to the wheels. Draw the windows. Add curved lines to the front of the car. Add lines to the hood. Add a line between the back ovals.

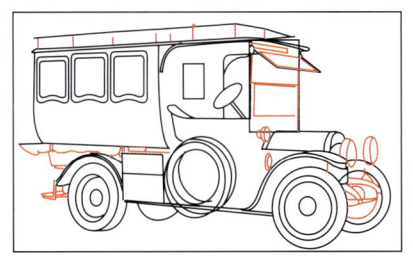

6

Erase the hood and window guides. Add vertical lines to the roof. Add the details to the window, the wheels, and the body of the ambulance. Add the circles for the headlights.

7

Using straight lines add spokes to the wheels. Draw the lines on the headlights, the hood, and the roof. Draw the four curved triangles on the side of the car.

8

Erase extra lines. Finish up the drawing by adding shading. Notice that the inside of the windows and parts of the wheels are the darkest. Nice work!

The Nobel Peace Prize

After the war ended, Wilson was honored with the Nobel Peace Prize. This is an award given to a person who has worked to support world peace. The Peace Prize medal, shown here, has a picture of Alfred Nobel on it. He established the prize in 1901. The peace prize was given to Wilson in 1919, for his plan to create an organization of nations that would settle conflicts between countries peacefully. That organization was called the League of Nations.

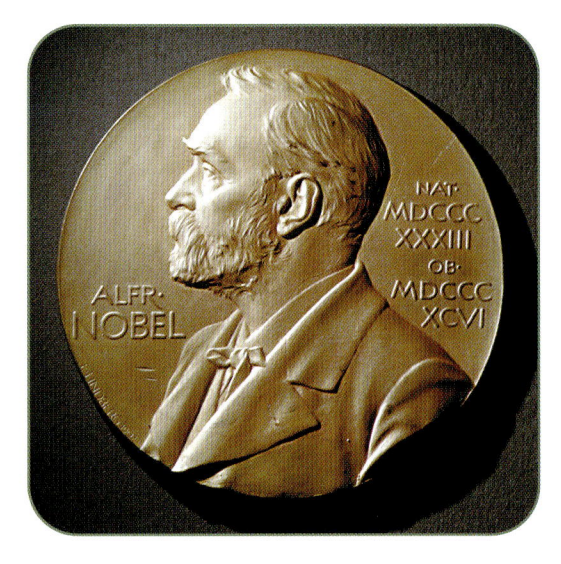

The League of Nations was part of Wilson's Fourteen Points speech. He gave this speech at a peace conference in Paris, France, in 1919.

After the League of Nations was established in 1919, the U.S. Congress voted against joining it. Wilson was disappointed because he believed that the League of Nations could help prevent future wars. Wilson's vision of America's participation in an international peace organization would be realized with the establishment of the United Nations in 1945.

1 You will be drawing the Nobel Peace Prize medal. Begin the drawing of the coin by drawing a square. Inside the square draw a circle, which will be the shape of the medal.

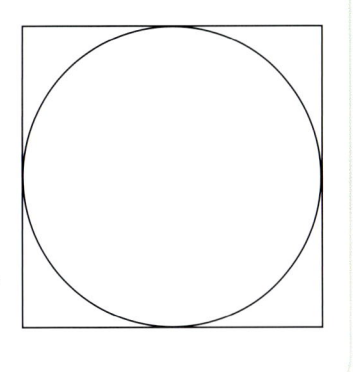

2 Draw a circular guide for the head and two slanted lines to make the guides for the body.

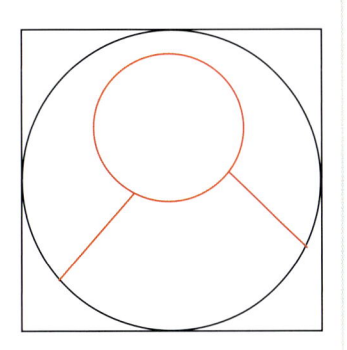

3 Using squiggly lines draw the outline of the hair, the face, and the body inside the guidelines you drew in step 2.

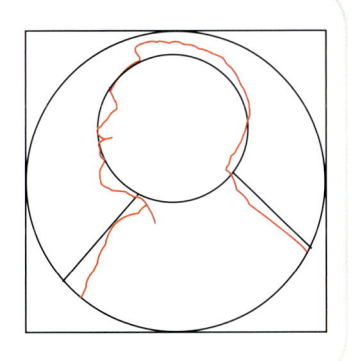

4 Using squiggly lines add the details for the hair, the beard, and the neck as shown. Draw slanted lines for the jacket.

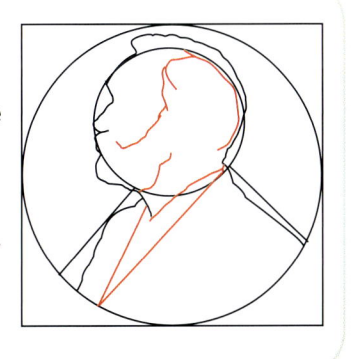

5 Erase the guidelines. Draw the jacket. Add an oval guide for the ear. Draw a guide for the bow tie. Using straight lines add the guides for the eye and the eyebrow.

6 Draw the ear. Draw the eyebrow. Finish the eye and nose. Add the lettering. The left side should read "ALFR. NOBEL." The right side should have the Latin words and numbers "NAT. MDCCC, XXXIII, OB. MDCCC, XCVI."

7 Erase the ear and eye guides. Using squiggly lines draw the hair. Draw the vest and the bow tie.

8 Erase extra lines. Finish by adding shading. Wonderful work!

Suffrage for Women

In 1920, Woodrow Wilson passed the Nineteenth Amendment to the U.S. Constitution. This amendment gave women suffrage, which means the right to vote.

The women's suffrage movement had begun in 1848, when women called suffragettes began to demand equal rights. Wilson's two daughters were suffragettes, but he did not address their cause in his 1912 presidential campaign. He was afraid that supporting women's suffrage would anger voters who were against it. If that happened, Wilson risked losing the election.

During his presidency the suffragettes tried many methods to win Wilson's support. They made posters, like the one above, to promote the cause. They protested in front of the White House, shown in the above photograph. Wilson was finally swayed by the suffragettes' actions and signed the Nineteenth Amendment in 1920.

1 You will be drawing a suffrage poster. Begin by drawing a rectangular guide. Next draw two circles. Add a small rectangle at the bottom. Connect the larger circle to the rectangle using vertical lines.

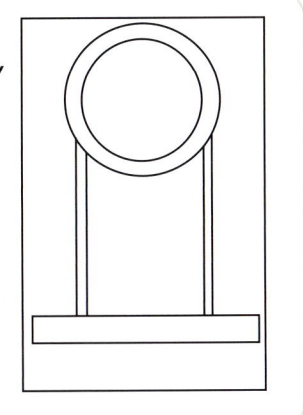

2 Draw curved lines on the bottom rectangle. Add an oval on the rectangle. Using straight lines draw a stick figure. Add guides for the hands and the eyes.

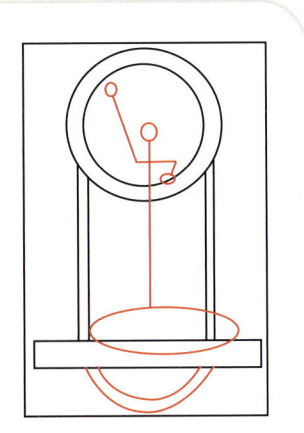

3 Draw long oval guides for the arms and body. Add a squiggly line inside the oval you drew in step 2. This will be the shape of the alligator's body.

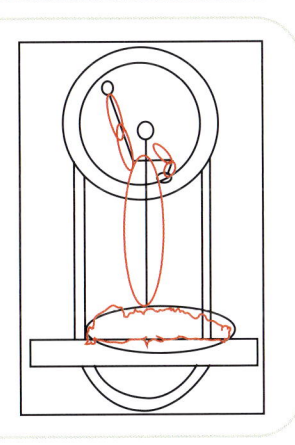

4 Erase the oval guideline. Using squiggly lines draw the shape of the head, hair, clothes, and body. Use the guide shapes you drew in step 3 to help you.

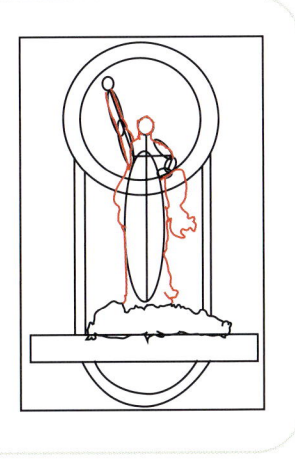

5 Erase extra lines. Using squiggly lines draw the hair. Add the shape of the torch using an oval and a rectangle. Draw straight lines along the edges of the poster.

6 Write the words "TRUTH LIBERTY JUSTICE" between the two circles. Write the words "VOTES FOR WOMEN" in the bottom rectangle. Draw six stars in the bottom curve. Add the details to lady liberty. Draw the alligator's tail.

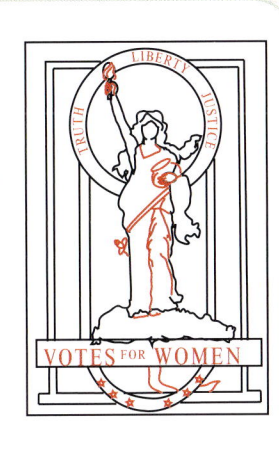

7 Erase the guide shapes for the torch and the hands. Add more details to the clothing using squiggly lines. Draw the face. Draw the alligator's face and add details to its body.

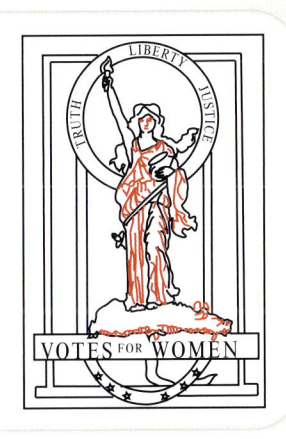

8 Erase the large rectangular guide you drew in step 1. Finish by adding detail and shading. Draw squiggly lines inside the circle for the globe. Add more lines around her body. Good job!

Wilson's Legacy

Wilson left the White House in 1921. He and Edith then retired to their new home in Washington, D.C. Because he had suffered a stroke two years before, Wilson was too ill to work at his law office. He died at home on February 3, 1924, at age 67.

Throughout his life Wilson loved to read and learn about new inventions and ideas. He was the first president to travel to Europe and the first to visit with the pope in Rome, Italy, while he was in office. Wilson left Americans with a legacy of legislation that improved their lives. The example Wilson set in this legislation and his work at promoting peace encouraged others to take part in public service.

Wilson is considered by historians to be one of the greatest American presidents. He fought hard for reforms in government, led America to victory during World War I, and helped create the League of Nations to promote peace.

1

Begin drawing Woodrow Wilson by making a rectangular guide. Add an oval for the head. Draw two slanted lines for the shoulder guides. Draw a vertical line down the center to make a guide for the body.

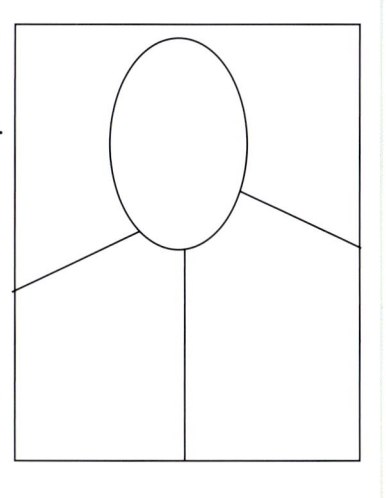

2

Draw two ovals for ear guides. Using straight lines draw the guides for the eyes, nose, and mouth. Using wavy lines draw the outline of Wilson's shoulders.

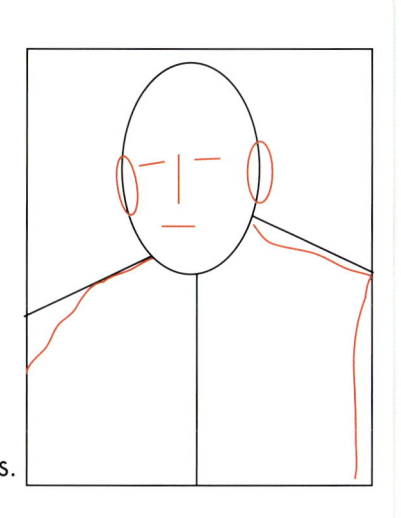

3

Erase extra lines. Use wavy lines to draw his hair. Use curved lines to draw the outline of his face and his ears. Add the lines for the jacket.

4

Erase the ear guides. Using wavy lines draw the eyes, nose, and mouth. Add more lines for the jacket, shirt, and vest.

5

Erase the head and face guides. Draw small circles for the pupils in the eyes. Add the eyebrows using curved lines. Add the remaining details to the face and the ear. Using wavy lines draw the lines for the shirt and tie.

6

Erase the rectangular guide you made in step 1. Finish your drawing by adding shading. Notice that the jacket and the tie are dark. Nice work!

Timeline

1856 Thomas Woodrow Wilson is born on December 28.

1873 Wilson enters Davidson College in North Carolina.

1875-1879 Wilson attends Princeton University in Princeton, New Jersey.

1885 Wilson marries Ellen Louise Axson.

1902 Wilson is elected president of Princeton University.

1910 Wilson is elected governor of New Jersey.

1912 Wilson is elected president of the United States.

1913 Wilson passes the Federal Reserve Act.
Wilson passes the Seventeenth Amendment.

1914 World War I begins in Europe.
Ellen Wilson dies on August 6.

1915 Wilson marries Edith Galt on December 18.

1916 Wilson is reelected president.

1917 Wilson asks Congress to declare war on Germany on April 2.

1918 World War I ends on November 11.

1919 Wilson passes the Eighteenth Amendment.
Wilson attends the Paris Peace Conference in Paris, France. He gives his Fourteen Points speech and pushes for the establishment of the League of Nations.
Wilson receives the Nobel Peace Prize.

1920 Wilson passes the Nineteenth Amendment.

1921 Wilson retires from the presidency.

1924 Wilson dies at home on February 3.

Glossary

alcohol (AL-kuh-hol) A liquid, such as beer or wine, that can make a person lose control or get drunk.

amendments (uh-MEND-ments) Additions or changes to the Constitution.

award (uh-WORD) A prize given to honor something.

Congress (KON-gres) The part of the U.S. government that makes laws.

conservative (kun-SER-vuh-tiv) Favoring keeping things as they are.

Constitution (kon-stuh-TOO-shun) The basic rules by which the United States is governed.

declare (dih-KLAYR) To announce officially.

demand (dih-MAND) To require something.

foundation (fown-DAY-shun) A group whose purpose is to take care of something.

lawyer (LOY-er) A person who gives advice about the law and who speaks for people in court.

legacy (LEH-guh-see) Something left behind by a person's actions.

legislatures (LEH-jis-lay-churz) Bodies of people that have the power to make or pass laws.

neutral (NOO-trul) On neither side of an argument or a war.

nominated (NAH-muh-nayt-ed) To have suggested that someone or something should be given an award or a position.

policy (PAH-lih-see) A law that people use to help them make decisions.

progressive (pruh-GREH-siv) Wanting to make changes in order to improve something.

promote (pruh-MOHT) To help spread an idea that a person believes is important.

reforms (rih-FORMZ) Changes or improvements.

rotunda (roh-TUN-duh) A round building, generally covered by a dome.

shrine (SHRYN) A special place built in honor of an important person.

stroke (STROHK) A medical condition that occurs when the brain does not receive oxygen.

submarines (SUB-muh-reenz) Ships that are designed to travel underwater.

surrendered (suh-REN-derd) Gave up.

Index

D
Davidson College, 4
Debs, Eugene, 16
Democratic Party, 5, 12

E
Eighteenth Amendment, 6

F
flu epidemic, 22
Fourteen Points speech, 6, 24

J
Johns Hopkins University, 5

L
League of Nations, 6, 24, 28

N
Nineteenth Amendment, 6, 26
Nobel Peace Prize, 24

P
Princeton University, 4–5, 12

R
Roosevelt, Franklin D., 10
Roosevelt, Theodore, 16

S
Seventeenth Amendment, 6

T
Taft, William, 16

Trotter, William, 18

U
United Nations, 24

W
Wilson, Edith Galt (second wife), 6, 28
Wilson, Ellen Louise Axson (first wife), 5, 6
Wilson, Janet Woodrow (mother), 4
Wilson, Joseph (father), 4
Woodrow Wilson Library, 10
World War I, 6, 20, 28

Web Sites

Due to the changing nature of Internet links, PowerKids Press has developed an online list of Web sites related to the subject of this book. This site is updated regularly. Please use this link to access the list:
www.powerkidslinks.com/kgdpusa/wilson/

MCDOUGLE ELEMENTARY
10410 Kansack Lane
Houston, Texas 77086